# JOHN D. ROCKEFELLER

# JOHN D.
# ROCKEFELLER
## ENTREPRENEUR & PHILANTHROPIST

### by Susan E. Hamen

Content Consultant:
Kenneth W. Rose, associate director of research & education
Rockefeller Archive Center

**ABDO**
Publishing Company

# CREDITS

Published by ABDO Publishing Company, 8000 West 78th Street, Edina, Minnesota 55439. Copyright © 2011 by Abdo Consulting Group, Inc. International copyrights reserved in all countries. No part of this book may be reproduced in any form without written permission from the publisher. The Essential Library™ is a trademark and logo of ABDO Publishing Company.

Printed in the United States of America,
North Mankato, Minnesota
112010
012011

 THIS BOOK CONTAINS AT LEAST 10% RECYCLED MATERIALS.

Editor: Amy Van Zee
Copy Editor: Karen Latchana Kenney
Interior Design and Production: Kazuko Collins
Cover Design: Kazuko Collins

**Library of Congress Cataloging-in-Publication Data**
Hamen, Susan E.
 John D. Rockefeller : entrepreneur & philanthropist / by Susan E. Hamen.
    p. cm. -- (Essential lives)
 Includes bibliographical references and index.
 ISBN 978-1-61714-784-5
 1. Rockefeller, John D. (John Davison), 1839-1937. 2. Businesspeople--United States--Biography. 3. Capitalists and financiers--United States--Biography. 4. Philanthropists--United States--Biography. I. Title.
 HC102.5.R548H36 2011
 338.7'622382092--dc22
 [B]
                                          2010042438

# TABLE OF CONTENTS

*John D. Rockefeller is remembered in history as an excellent
businessman and a generous philanthropist.*

# YOUNG DETERMINATION

*I*n 1855, Cleveland, Ohio, was a rest
stop for those Americans adventurous
enough to try their hand out West. The city bustled
with a population of nearly 30,000 residents. An
additional few thousand travelers filled the city's

numerous boardinghouses before continuing on to the farmlands of the West and the gold mines of California. German and English settlers poured into Cleveland. This boomtown was an exciting place for any young man.

In mid-August 1855, it was particularly sweltering as one young man came to Cleveland. At the height of the summer's heat, 16-year-old John D. Rockefeller returned to Cleveland after a month-long vacation at his family's home 13 miles (21 km) outside the city.

Young Rockefeller had one goal: to secure a position as a bookkeeper in one of the city's most distinguished businesses. He created a list of Cleveland's biggest, most prominent companies, including banks, railroad offices, shipping firms, and commission houses. He later explained, "I did not guess what it would be, but I was after something big."[1]

The tall, thin boy with piercing blue eyes faced difficult odds. The expanding city attracted numerous young men who were hunting for work. Rockefeller knew no one of importance in Cleveland who might help him land a job. He did not have any letters of recommendation to show a possible employer. He had nothing but his determination to find the position he so desperately desired.

## The Daily Routine

Rockefeller lived in a small room in a boardinghouse. He woke early each morning. After breakfast, he dressed in his dark suit and black tie, making sure to look professional. Then he left the boardinghouse at 8:00 a.m. Six days a week, Monday through Saturday, Rockefeller walked the hard, hot streets of Cleveland in pursuit of work. He stopped at the

### A Booming Town

In the 1850s, Cleveland was growing steadily. European immigrants arrived seeking better futures in the promising city. They brought with them skills and trades that helped bolster Cleveland as a center of industry.

The Cuyahoga River wound its way through the city past roaring lumber mills, iron foundries, warehouses, and shipyards, and emptied into Lake Erie, one of the five Great Lakes. Steamboats and schooners crowded the wharves, carrying goods and commodities to and from Cleveland. The arrival of the Cleveland, Columbus and Cincinnati Railroad in 1851 further expanded the city's transportation routes. Cleveland had become the port through which the bounty of the Midwest traveled on its way to other areas of the United States.

The city lacked paved roads, but it was host to three daily newspapers, including the African-American newspaper *The Aliened-American*, which began publication in April 1853.

Cultural and educational establishments sprouted up as well. Cleveland University and Cleveland Medical College offered opportunities for higher learning. The Globe Theater, the Cleveland Theater, and the Cleveland Library Association provided the city's cultural events.

businesses on his list, one after the next, politely asking to speak to the man in charge. He got straight to the point. "I understand bookkeeping, and I'd like to get work," he confidently stated.[2]

But no businesses were interested in hiring a young man without experience. Still, Rockefeller continued on his rounds, revisiting the same businesses after he had gone through his entire list. His trek lasted all day until the offices closed. As Rockefeller explained, "I was working every day at my business—the business of looking for work. I put in my full time at this every day."[3]

He turned down his father's offer to return home to the country to be supported by his parents. The growing city held unlimited potential for a diligent young businessman, if only Rockefeller could get his foot in the door. Cleveland had become a hub of transportation. The wharves of Lake Erie teemed with schooners and paddle steamers that carried produce from the Midwest and products from the East Coast brought through the Erie Canal. Pennsylvania

**What If?**

"No one wanted a boy, and very few showed any overwhelming anxiety to talk with me on the subject," Rockefeller recalled about his job hunt. He later said about the day he was hired at Hewitt and Tuttle, "All my future seemed to hinge on that day; and I often tremble when I ask myself the question: 'What if I had not got the job?'"[4]

*Cleveland, Ohio, was growing as an industrial city
in the mid-nineteenth century.*

coal, Michigan salt, and Minnesota iron ore passed
through Cleveland. If one firm would simply give
him a chance, Rockefeller was confident he would be
successful.

## A Foot in the Door

On the morning of September 26, 1855, after
six weeks of canvassing for a position, Rockefeller
entered the offices of Hewitt and Tuttle on Merwin
Street. The partners ran a produce-shipping
business and a commission office—a company that

works as a middleman between buyers and sellers. As luck would have it, junior partner Henry B. Tuttle was in need of bookkeeping help. He interviewed Rockefeller and asked him to return after lunch. Rockefeller calmly left the office, but once around the corner, he skipped down the street. Finally, he was close to realizing his goal.

When Rockefeller returned later in the day, senior partner Isaac L. Hewitt inspected Rockefeller's penmanship. Because everything was recorded by hand, it was imperative that the books were neat and easily legible. Many bookkeepers of the day wrote in the copperplate fashion. This neat, elegant style of cursive handwriting was used by bookkeepers, lawyers, and businessmen.

Senior partner Hewitt thought the young man deserved a chance. The partners asked Rockefeller to hang up his coat and begin work immediately in an apprenticeship of sorts. Neither Hewitt nor Tuttle informed Rockefeller what his wage

**Humble Beginnings**

Rockefeller's illustrious career began with him sitting on a high stool bent over a musty ledger in a room lit by a whale-oil lamp. He was delighted. "As I began my life as a bookkeeper, I learned to have great respect for figures and facts, no matter how small they were. . . . I had a passion for detail which afterward I was forced to strive to modify," he recalled.[5]

would be. Rockefeller later said he did not care—any amount would do. Rockefeller was not even paid until he had worked for three months.

As it turned out, the man who would go on to become America's first billionaire began his renowned career by earning a few dollars a week as an assistant bookkeeper. Until his dying day, John D. Rockefeller celebrated September 26, the day he was hired, as Job Day. No matter where he and his family were, the American flag was raised and everyone enjoyed a celebration feast. He regarded Job Day as being more important than his own birthday. But in 1855, as Rockefeller sat on his bookkeeper's stool in the office of Hewitt and Tuttle, he did not know that his name would one day become synonymous with extravagant wealth.

**A Mind for Numbers**

Rockefeller called the opportunity at Hewitt and Tuttle a "gentleman's position."[6] Well before the age of the modern calculator, a bookkeeper had to have a good head for numbers. It was perfect for Rockefeller, who had excelled at arithmetic during his school years.

*Rockefeller in 1930*

*William Avery Rockefeller*

# THE YOUNG ENTREPRENEUR

John Davison Rockefeller was born on July 8, 1839, in the family cottage near Richford, New York. He was the second child of William Avery "Big Bill" Rockefeller and Eliza Davison Rockefeller. He was named after John

Davison, his mother's father. John had an older
sister, Lucy, and younger siblings William, Mary
Ann, and twins Franklin and Francis. Francis died as
an infant, but the remaining children lived long lives.

The first three Rockefeller children were born
in a small home their father Big Bill had built half a
mile (.8 km) from his parents' home. Set on a slope
overlooking rolling hills, the house was situated on
a 50-acre (20-ha) lot. It was also home to a small
apple orchard and the Owego Creek, which ran
through the property and provided much bounty for
trout fishing.

## THE ROCKEFELLER FAMILY

Big Bill was a traveling pitchman
and was often on the road. He was
a "flimflam man"—someone who
traveled the countryside claiming
to be a doctor and peddling
fake remedies for all manner of
illnesses, including cancer. Many
of these so-called remedies were
merely alcohol with added vegetable
extracts or morphine and had no
true medicinal properties. Big Bill

### Traveling Doctors and Medicines

Today's Food and Drug Administration tests and approves medicines before they can be sold to the public. But Big Bill's homemade remedies were not tested for safety or effectiveness.

In truth, the vast majority of the medicines sold by traveling salesmen were not only phony, but several of them were dangerous to consume. Some contained alcohol, cocaine, or even opium.

charged up to $25 for a bottle of his cure-all medicine.

Big Bill was a tall, broad-shouldered man who loved to bluff and tell tall tales. Eliza was a straitlaced farm girl with delicate features, blue eyes, and flaming red hair. She was raised as a strict Baptist, but her one vice was smoking her corncob pipe. She was intrigued by William, the flashy flimflam man. Ironically, when Eliza was 12, her mother had died after taking a pill sold by a traveling doctor. Eliza was drawn in by William's charisma. Against her father's wishes, she married William on February 18, 1837.

### Big Bill's Charm

How did Big Bill meet his wife, Eliza? The story was told that Big Bill came to Eliza's father's house selling his quack medicines. He could easily charm and beguile most people he met, and this day, he employed a special method of winning the affection of others. He pretended to be deaf and mute, using a small slate chalkboard to communicate with his potential customers. This ploy often played on people's sympathy and helped him sell more of his herbal remedies.

Upon seeing the supposed deaf and mute salesman at the door, 24-year-old Eliza was reported as saying, "If that man were not deaf and dumb, I'd marry him."[1] Upon discovering that Bill could, in fact, hear and talk, Eliza soon fell for the smooth-talking con artist.

As a married woman, Eliza's home life was difficult. She was often left to look after the family's large, 50-acre (20-ha) farm. While Eliza spent her days working hard to keep family and home together, Big Bill traveled great distances to peddle his potions and work on other moneymaking schemes.

## LIFE ON THE FARM

Eliza's dreams of a romantic life with Big Bill were short lived. He left Eliza in charge of the children, the household, and their large farm while he traveled for months at a time. He returned periodically with large sums of money, wearing fancy clothing, and riding fine horses. During his absences, Eliza bought necessary supplies for the family on credit at the general store. She never knew when the store owner would cut her off or when Big Bill would return to settle the bill.

When Big Bill was at home, he would spend time with John and the other children. He taught them to shoot, swim, and deal in business. John later recalled that it was his father who taught him to write a loan note and instilled in him the importance of paying off debts. John was also taught that contracts should be honored by both buyer and seller and that personal feelings should not enter into the deal.

Young John may have learned business sense from his father, but he owed his hard work, discipline, and determination to his mother. In 1843, Big Bill and Eliza moved the family to a 92-acre (37-ha) farm. It was just three miles (4.8 km) from Eliza's family on the outskirts of

*William and Eliza Rockefeller's children:* from left,
John, Lucy, Mary Ann, Frank, and William

Moravia. Eliza assigned farm chores to the children
and again kept the farm going while her husband
was away.

## MAKING MONEY

John started at a young age with his own
moneymaking ideas. At seven, he followed a wild
turkey hen to her nest in the woods and swiped her
eggs. With his mother's help, he raised the chicks,
which he then sold. John also discovered that if he
bought candy by the pound, he could make money by
selling it in smaller portions to his siblings.

He kept his earnings in a small blue china bowl on the family's mantel. Eliza instilled in her children a staunch sense of duty to the Baptist church. Every Sunday morning, she and the children attended services, and the children would drop a portion of their earnings into the collection plate.

John attended school in a white, one-room schoolhouse that his father helped establish. He had to work hard to get only decent grades, but his patience and perseverance made up for what he lacked in natural ability. He developed a good head for math and numbers and was known for carefully thinking through problems.

As Big Bill continued to travel for months at a time, he earned a reputation as a womanizer. In 1849, charges of rape were brought against him. Bill and Eliza moved the family to Owego, a city close to the Pennsylvania border, presumably to avoid a trial. Although nothing became of the charges, Eliza's image of her husband changed. She began to rely more upon her eldest son, John.

**Giving**

About saving and giving, Rockefeller later noted, "I was trained from the beginning to work and to save. I have always regarded it as a religious duty to get all I could honorably and to give all I could."[2] He considered his mother's insistence on giving to be the reason for his philanthropic deeds later in life.

In Owego, John threw himself into work while not in school. He helped his mother keep accurate accounts of the family budget and performed manual chores around the farmstead. John had the opportunity to work for a neighboring farmer digging potatoes for 37.5¢ a day. Not long after, a different farmer borrowed $50 from John at a 7 percent interest rate—an additional fee for borrowing money that is paid back to the lender along with the original sum. By the end of the year, when the loan came due, John collected the $50 plus $3.50 in interest. The young boy was astonished that he had made more profit by allowing his money to work for him than he had earned spending three whole days digging potatoes. In 1904, he commented, "The impression was gaining ground with me that it was a good thing to let the money be my servant and not make myself a slave to the money."[3]

## A Fine Education

In August 1852, John began classes at the Owego Academy with his brother William. The academy was known to be the finest secondary school in the region, and John worked hard at his studies. With

tuition at three dollars per semester, it was a struggle
for John's family to send the boys to the school.
John and William were some of the poorer students
attending Owego Academy.

In 1853, Big Bill moved Eliza and the five children
to a farm not far from Cleveland, Ohio. Around that
time, he began courting another woman, 17-year-old
Margaret Allen, who lived in Ontario, Canada. By
this time, he was traveling and peddling his potions
under the false name of Dr. William Levingston. Miss
Allen and her family, impressed by "Dr. Levingston,"
knew nothing of the Rockefeller family in Cleveland.
Big Bill, at age 42, married the unknowing teenager
on June 12, 1855, in Nichols, New York, and began
an intricate double life. Eliza never learned of
Margaret Allen.

In the fall of 1853, when John was
14, Big Bill drove him to Cleveland.
He enrolled John in school there,
opened a bank account for him, and
set him up in a boardinghouse on Erie
Street. John attended the Clinton
Street School and then Central High
School, where he showed aptitude for
math and debating.

**A Teacher Remembers**

John's tutor remembered,
"I have no recollection of
John excelling at anything.
I do remember he worked
hard at everything: not
talking much, and study-
ing with great industry. . . .
There was nothing about
him to make anybody pay
especial attention to him
or speculate about his
future."[4]

**Family Resemblance**

John resembled his mother physically. They had the same delicate features and the same intense blue eyes. Like his mother, John rarely lost his temper or raised his voice.

Left on his own, John took to his studies with his usual serious demeanor. He attended the Erie Street Baptist Church (which later became the Euclid Avenue Baptist Church) and was baptized in 1854. He attended two church services on Sundays and Friday prayer meetings. The members of the church, mostly working-class families, made him feel welcome in the big city. Most of the friends he made in Cleveland were from church.

John felt pressure from his father to drop out of high school to take business courses, which he did in 1855. It was just two months before his graduation. John paid $40 to attend a ten-week series of courses at Folsom's Commercial College. He learned the finer points of bookkeeping, banking, mercantile customs, and penmanship. The courses prepared him for employment as a bookkeeper.

After completing the business courses, John returned to the family home in the country for one month, where he celebrated his sixteenth birthday. He prepared himself for his return to Cleveland, where he would seek out a job with a distinguished firm.

*John's mother, Eliza Davison Rockefeller*

*Young Rockefeller*

# THE SAVVY BUSINESSMAN

Cleveland grew as a transportation hub, and commodities such as grains, beef, pork, and salt made their way through the city either by railroad or water. Hewitt and Tuttle arranged the buying and selling of commodities between a wholesaler, such as a farmer selling his grain or livestock, and a buyer, such as a store wanting to sell the farmer's products to consumers. They would then organize the transportation of and payments for the products, charging a commission, or fee, for doing so.

Commission houses used the telegraph to keep current on the daily prices of commodities, which allowed them to calculate rates. At times, commission houses would buy entire shipments outright and then find buyers for the commodity, usually turning large profits in the process.

## AN EXCELLENT REPUTATION

Rockefeller settled into a rigorous routine as bookkeeper for Hewitt and Tuttle. He arrived at the office at 6:30 a.m. and often worked into the night, breaking only for supper. Rockefeller thoroughly checked and rechecked the ledgers, passionately making sure every neat entry was correct. Mr. Tuttle retired in January 1857, and Rockefeller took Tuttle's duties. He soon gained a reputation for being a thorough, strict accountant. "I scrutinized every bill. If it had ever so many items, I went over each one, verified it, and carefully added the

**Rockefeller and the Euclid Avenue Baptist Church**

The Euclid Avenue Baptist Church became a central point in Rockefeller's life. During his high school days, he served the church as a Sunday school teacher. Later, he served as a trustee and recorded board-meeting minutes. When the church was at risk for foreclosure, Rockefeller put his business skills to work and persuaded each member to pledge money to pay off the $2,000 debt. Within months, he had saved the church.

totals. The bill had to be accurate in every detail before I okayed it to be paid," he explained.[1] Clients would sometimes prod him to simply round up or down, but Rockefeller was accurate to the penny in his business dealings. He argued that if he was dishonest with even one person, he could not be trusted by anyone.

In addition to keeping the books at Hewitt and Tuttle, Rockefeller kept careful track of every penny of his own money that he spent. His personal ledger detailed every expense and every charitable gift he gave, most of which went to the Baptist church.

During his three years at Hewitt and Tuttle, Rockefeller learned the ways that commission houses, railroads, and barges worked together. Savvy businessmen were able to negotiate prices for water shipments, and Rockefeller became experienced in working out settlements for late or damaged shipments. He also learned that the railroads were willing to charge fixed rates for shipping, and then issue rebates at the end of the month to their best customers. These opportunities put more profits in the pockets of the commission house.

It was also during his tenure at Hewitt and Tuttle that Rockefeller developed his style of collecting debts owed to his employer. Whereas many debt collectors used intimidation or demands, Rockefeller kept a cool head. He persistently reasoned with the debtor until he got his way.

## A New Home

In 1857, Big Bill moved his family to Cleveland. He purchased a lot on Cheshire Street and left money to build a house. He put John in charge of the project and left. The Rockefellers still had no knowledge of Big Bill's double life.

Only 18, young Rockefeller oversaw

### Ledger A

When Rockefeller was hired at Hewitt and Tuttle, he purchased a small red personal ledger for 10¢. In it he recorded all of his expenditures. He named it Ledger A, and it became his most prized possession for the remainder of his life. In the book, he neatly and diligently kept track of every penny he spent or donated. When he filled the pages of Ledger A, Rockefeller purchased a new one and named it Ledger B, and so on.

For the rest of his life, Rockefeller kept meticulous records of his earnings, expenditures, and donations in ledgers. He would later insist that his children keep detailed ledgers of their money as well.

More than 40 years after its purchase, he showed Ledger A to a Bible class in 1897. Speculating on its personal worth, he emotionally explained, "You couldn't get it from me for all the modern ledgers in New York and what they all would bring in."[2]

the building of the house and held the contractor accountable for every expense. It did not take long for the contractor to realize there would be no cutting corners under Rockefeller's watchful eye. The result was a beautiful house at a reasonable price.

## A Partnership Blooms

After three years, when Rockefeller was effectively running most aspects of Hewitt and Tuttle, he was earning approximately $600 a year. He submitted his resignation with the intention of opening up his own commission house. Shortly after Rockefeller quit, Hewitt and Tuttle went out of business.

At age 19, Rockefeller entered into business with Maurice B. Clark, a 28-year-old English immigrant whom Rockefeller met at Folsom's Commercial College. Clark had $2,000 to put into the partnership and asked Rockefeller if he could do the same. Rockefeller had managed to save $800 from his wages at Hewitt and Tuttle. His father advanced him $1,000, a sum he intended to give each of his children upon their twenty-first birthdays.

### Help for Eliza

By 1857, Big Bill abandoned Eliza, who had essentially raised five children on her own. When Eliza's father died on June 1, 1858, he left her an annuity that would offer a source of income for years to come. She also relied heavily upon John, who was always a steadfast support to her.

Big Bill charged a 10 percent interest rate. Young Rockefeller would pay the interest until he reached age 21. By combining their money, the two men were able to open the commission house of Clark and Rockefeller in the spring of 1859.

While Rockefeller handled the books and the money in the office, Clark toured the countryside in search of customers. The two men felt that to be successful, they had to be competitive. They began offering larger advances on crops. They offered to pay more money to farmers up front, before Rockefeller and Clark actually sold the crops. This offer benefited farmers by putting money quickly back in their hands.

Since Clark and Rockefeller were paying out before profits were coming in, they needed another way to bring in money. Their only option was to take out loans. Rockefeller

**The "Angola Horror"**

Rockefeller was known as a punctual man. But a late start on the morning of December 18, 1867, might have saved his life.

Rockefeller planned to travel from Cleveland to New York City to wrap up some business items before the Christmas holiday. He packed and headed for the train station, intending to catch a 6:40 a.m. train to Buffalo. He was running late, and while his luggage was loaded onto the train, Rockefeller was not.

He caught the next train to Buffalo, which was delayed partway through its journey. The last two cars of the 6:40 a.m. train—which Rockefeller intended to travel on—had derailed and crashed into a river gorge near the city of Angola, New York. Almost 50 people died. Because he was running late, it is likely that Rockefeller would have sat in one of the back cars that had crashed. The crash became known as the "Angola Horror."

again turned to his father. But soon, Rockefeller needed more money than his father could offer.

With his reputation as a fair and trustworthy businessman, Rockefeller turned to the Cleveland banks instead. Truman P. Handy, president of the bank at which Rockefeller and his partner held their accounts, agreed to loan the young man $2,000. Rockefeller never forgot Mr. Handy's trust in him at such a young age. "Just think of it, a bank had trusted me for $2,000! I felt that I was now a man of importance in the community," he remembered.[3]

Rockefeller continued exercising his natural business abilities and the firm soon grew. He sought more and more loans from Cleveland banks in order to expand the business. If he was turned down by a bank president, he simply went to another bank, explaining later, "That made no difference to me; simply meant that I must look elsewhere until I got what I wanted."[4]

During their first year, the partners of Clark and Rockefeller did almost $500,000 in business, profiting $4,400. The following year, the men pocketed $17,500. ⌒

3

| 1855 | Donations | | |
|---|---|---|---|
| Nov | 25 | To Missionary Cause | 15 |
| | " | Mr Downey | 10 |
| | " | Mite Society | 75 |
| | " | Slip Rent | — |
| Dec | 15 | Sabath School Contribu— | 05 |
| | 23 | present for Mr Fair— | 25 |
| | 30 | Five Point Mission | 12 |
| | " | Macedonian | 10 |
| | " | Present to Town Shed | 25 |
| Jany | 6 | Missionary Cause | 06 |
| | " | the poor in the church | 10 |
| Feby | 3 | " " " " | 10 |
| | " | Foreign Mission | 10 |
| Mar | 2 | Do | 10 |
| | " | poor in the Church | 10 |
| | " | Slip Rent to May 1 | 1. |
| | | Amt for | 4 33 |

*A page from Rockefeller's Ledger A*

*Approximately 90,000 Union troops fought in the Battle of Gettysburg. The American Civil War brought business to Rockefeller as the troops needed supplies.*

# THE BUSINESS OF OIL

Rockefeller continued to work six days a week at the commission house, fervently trying to increase business. Because space on railroad cars was limited during harvest season, the task of securing transportation for his consignments was tricky. The persistent young man was not intimidated, though.

Rockefeller and Clark did not always agree on how to run the business. Clark was looking for a stable, secure income. Rockefeller, on the other hand, wanted to turn the commission house into a huge success. Clark disapproved of the large loans the younger partner was taking out, stating Rockefeller was "the greatest borrower you ever saw."[1]

Although nine years younger than his partner, Rockefeller soon felt that he was responsible for the success of the business. He wanted to prove that he could be just as successful performing his partner's work. So, Rockefeller began traveling the countryside as well, seeking out customers—something only Clark had been doing. Despite their different business philosophies, the two men continued working as partners.

## Civil War Erupts

In 1861, the American Civil War broke out. Clark and Rockefeller soon found it had a positive effect on their business. The Union army required large amounts of food and supplies, and the commissions began rolling in.

As the Civil War continued, Rockefeller continued working steadfastly. His younger brother Frank, only 16, had joined the Union army. Feeling he could not pull himself from his professional responsibilities, Rockefeller did not join the cause, but he sent money to help outfit the soldiers with weapons and supplies.

## OIL DISCOVERED

A few years before the war broke out, a discovery was made that drastically affected not only Rockefeller's business but also the US economy as a whole. On August 27, 1859, Colonel Edwin L. Drake successfully drilled into a large reserve of crude oil, or petroleum, in Titusville, Pennsylvania. After a process called refining, this crude oil could burn as cleanly as kerosene, an oil used in lamps. Prior to this, kerosene was extracted only from coal and involved expensive, lengthy processes. The new crude oil kerosene was much cheaper, and many people were eager to buy it.

### A Clever Trick

During the Civil War, many young men were drafted to serve in the Union army. However, the Conscription Act made it legal for a draftee to avoid service by paying $300, which Rockefeller did.

Rockefeller's youngest brother, Frank, was eager to join the army but was too young. So that he would not technically be lying, he wrote the number 18 on the soles of his boots with chalk. When the recruiting sergeant asked him his age, he replied, "I'm over eighteen, sir."[2]

*Colonel Edwin L. Drake, right, stands in front of his oil well in Pennsylvania in 1859.*

Prospectors flocked to the Oil Region of northwest Pennsylvania, particularly Titusville. Wells were dug and oil derricks constructed. Refineries sprang up in Pittsburgh, New York, and Cleveland. The "black gold," as it was called, was shipped in barrels by railroad cars to refineries. As the number of oil wells increased, and therefore the oil supply, the price of crude oil dropped. Yet, even with the cost of drilling, refining, and transporting it, there was still potential for a large profit margin in oil.

Commission houses soon took notice of this new oil business. They were well experienced in shipping products and monitoring fluctuating daily market prices. Although drilling continued at a rapid pace, no one could be certain that the supply of crude oil in Pennsylvania would hold out. Daily amounts of pumped oil were extremely unpredictable,

## A New Use for Crude Oil

Prior to crude oil kerosene, most people used candles or whale-oil lamps for light. But candles, with their dangerous and messy drips, were less than ideal. Whale oil, made from the blubber of certain species of whales, left a sooty residue when burned. Whaling had taken a toll on the whale population, and whale fisheries were not able to keep up with demand. This drove up the price of whale oil.

The discovery of crude oil answered the need for a cheap source of illumination. For years, crude oil bubbled up from the earth and could be skimmed off the water's surface. Native Americans used it as a medicine for stiff joints and headaches. They sold it to European settlers, calling it Seneca Oil.

The discovery of the refining process opened the door for a cheap, new lamp oil. Homes and shops around the world had a new, affordable option to candles and expensive whale-oil lamps.

Kerosene became the biggest use for crude oil until another discovery years later. The internal combustion engine, and then the automobile, would find a new use for crude oil. It would drive the demand for crude oil to unparalleled rates.

causing fluctuations in the railroad's business as well as in the price of crude oil. Instead of jumping into this new, questionable venture, Rockefeller decided to watch the oil business for a while.

Rockefeller visited the Oil Region to do some research. He soon decided that the financial potential did not lie in drilling, but in refining and distributing the kerosene. Before making any moves, Rockefeller waited and watched as the chaotic, new business settled down.

## A CHANGE IN BUSINESS

Rockefeller soon saw oil refineries being built along the rail lines, making transportation accessible and easy. Samuel Andrews, another English immigrant to Cleveland, approached Clark and Rockefeller in 1863. Andrews, a self-taught chemist, had built a refinery he believed to be of superior quality. But he knew nothing of business and transporting goods. He turned to the two-man team for help.

Rockefeller agreed to use some of his own cash to back Andrews. Clark then followed suit, saying, "Well, if John will go in I will."[3] Jim Clark, Maurice's brother, joined the venture. It was

When Edwin L. Drake successfully drilled for oil in 1859, he spawned a mass rush of people to the area looking to get rich quick. These "boomers," as they were called, set up oil derricks and began tapping into the oil supply. One of these boomers was a handsome actor named John Wilkes Booth. Later, he would be remembered in history as the man who shot and killed President Abraham Lincoln.

Andrews's job to operate the refinery. Rockefeller and Maurice Clark were simply silent partners who invested $4,000 in the new oil company. Andrews, Clark and Company was in business, and thus Rockefeller began his oil career at the age of 24.

Rockefeller later recounted that he and Maurice considered their $4,000 investment as, "seem[ing] very large to us, *very large.*"[4] They did not believe their second business would outgrow their commission house. "[It was] a little side issue, we retaining our interest in our business as produce commission merchants," he explained.[5] Rockefeller surely could not have imagined at the time where the oil business would lead him.

## Love Comes Calling

By age 24, Rockefeller was one of the most successful businessmen in Cleveland. He was respected and admired both in the business community of Cleveland and at his church. Those who knew Rockefeller commented that he was an intent, patient listener who spoke to people in a pleasant, friendly manner and kept his temper in check.

The Cleveland bachelor also had a love interest. His fellow classmate from Central High School, Laura Celestia Spelman, was the daughter of one of Cleveland's successful businessmen who also served as an Ohio state legislator. After graduation, she continued her education at Oread Collegiate Institute in Worcester, Massachusetts.

Cettie, as Laura's family and friends called her, was well educated and had written for her college newspaper. She returned to Cleveland to teach, where she and her father both became strong supporters of African-American rights. Her father helped slaves escape the South by way of the Underground Railroad. Cettie was also a firm supporter of outlawing alcohol and crusaded with her family throughout the temperance movement.

With dark eyes and long, chestnut hair, Cettie was as attractive as she was smart. Rockefeller was drawn to the quiet, intelligent valedictorian of their high school class. She was as active as Rockefeller in her church, and the two shared the same ideas about morality and responsible living.

Nine years after they met at Central High School, the two were married on September 8, 1864, in her parents' living room. Their engagement had lasted six months, beginning the day John spent a whopping $118 on a diamond engagement ring for Cettie. He carefully recorded all the expenses of their courting and wedding in his ledger. Ever the businessman, Rockefeller went to the office and worked the morning of his wedding day prior to the ceremony.

The newlyweds spent one month honeymooning in Niagara Falls, Montreal, and New England. Upon their return, they lived with Eliza for six months until moving into a two-story brick house down the road at 29 Cheshire Street. Cettie joined her husband at the Euclid Avenue Baptist Church.

Rockefeller valued Cettie's opinion and often discussed business matters with her. She checked his business letters for spelling mistakes and gladly offered her opinion whenever asked. With Cettie running the home, thriftily devoid of servants, Rockefeller continued to concentrate on his work.

**Cettie and John**

Cettie Rockefeller was a smart young woman. Like her husband, she was also dedicated to her church. Her sister remembered, "God and church came first with her. She cared little for the 'social life,' so called; and together she and her husband deepened and expanded their religion to cover and include every phase of life."[6]

*Laura Celestia Spelman*

*Rockefeller in 1865*

# Standard Oil Is Born

Rockefeller and his partners were wealthy men. But as the war came to an end in the mid-1860s, the need for supplies to the troops decreased—and so did the commission house's hefty profits. Rockefeller started believing that the oil

business held more promise than
he had initially thought. He was not
entirely satisfied with the way things
were going with Andrews, Clark and
Company, though.

## TENSION AND TACTICS

Maurice Clark had never fully
supported his partner's practice of
borrowing large sums of money,
and he was vocal in his complaints.
Rockefeller disagreed and strongly
believed it was the only way to drive
business. Rockefeller took on a more
active role in Andrews, Clark and
Company.

Rockefeller believed that key
improvements in the way their
refinery ran would cut costs

eventually, and he borrowed heavily to make those
costly changes happen. For example, he hired a
full-time plumber instead of hiring one every time
a repair was needed. Practices such as these did save
money for the company, but Clark believed the
start-up costs were too high.

The tension between Clark and Rockefeller continued to escalate. Rockefeller was also displeased with Clark's brother, Jim. Rockefeller, who never made a business decision without thoroughly researching the risk, thought Jim was not careful or methodical enough in his oil-buying decisions. He also thought Jim Clark was an immoral man. Rockefeller told Samuel Andrews that he wanted to split from the Clarks. Andrews agreed and reassured Rockefeller that should the business break up, he would be on Rockefeller's side.

## ROCKEFELLER MAKES HIS MOVE

Rockefeller got his personal finances in order, verified that his credit was still good with the banks in Cleveland, and made sure his outside investments in other business ventures were substantial enough to support his family should his new gamble fail. Then he proceeded to force dissolution of the company he had helped create.

The four men met in February 1865, agreeing to dissolve Andrews,

**Business Experience**

Rockefeller recalled that the early days of his oil business were full of "stress and strain, full of care, full of anxiety, it is true, and yet full of happiness that words cannot express: happiness because we were accomplishing from the earliest of our business experience, we were triumphing over the difficulties; we were being strengthened and prepared to meet the larger responsibilities."[1]

Clark and Company. The business would go to the highest bidder—Rockefeller or the Clarks. The Clark brothers, however, were certain that Andrews would be on their side. They were shocked to learn that he was siding with Rockefeller.

The Clarks hired an attorney to represent them at the auction. Representing himself and Andrews, Rockefeller felt the transaction would be simple. Bidding began at $500 and rose slowly to $50,000. When it hit $70,000, Rockefeller worried he would not be able to afford to buy the business. But after a bid of $72,000 from his opponents, Rockefeller made the final, winning bid of $72,500.

Rockefeller was now the owner of Cleveland's largest refinery. The Clark brothers were shocked that 25-year-old Rockefeller had successfully financed such a purchase. Of the experience, Rockefeller told an acquaintance in later years, "It was the day that determined my career. I felt the bigness of it, but I was as calm as I am talking to you now."[2]

## REARRANGING THE BUSINESS

Rockefeller renamed the company Rockefeller and Andrews in 1865. Rockefeller then plunged into learning everything he could about the oil business. He foresaw that Cleveland was at a disadvantage over the other three refinery areas in the United States: the Oil Region, Pittsburgh, and New York, all of which were closer to the oil derricks, and therefore required less rail transit. They were also closer to the Atlantic, making exportation abroad easier.

Rockefeller traveled to the Oil Region to learn about the drilling process. He asked questions and discussed procedures with pipeline owners, crude oil buyers,

### "Millionaires' Row"

In 1868, John and Cettie moved from their house on Cheshire Street to a brick house on Euclid Avenue. They raised their four daughters and one son there: Elizabeth ("Bessie") (1866), Alice (1869), Alta (1871), Edith (1872), and John Jr. (1874). Their second child, Alice, died as an infant.

Most of the homes on Euclid Avenue were lavish mansions with manicured lawns and gardens. The richest men in Cleveland were the Rockefellers' neighbors—men whose fortunes were made in oil, railroads, real estate, and banking. The mansions on Euclid Avenue earned the street the nickname "Millionaires' Row." Rockefeller's house, which he bought for $40,000, was beautiful and roomy, but less grandiose than others on the street. Although he could have afforded a much more expensive home, he did not see the need to flaunt his wealth.

However, the family also owned a large summer house in the country, where they enjoyed simple pleasures such as swimming and picnics. John and Cettie's social life still consisted of activities with the Euclid Avenue Baptist Church. Rockefeller considered himself a country boy at heart and found no need for "uppity" social clubs.

and railroad men. When he returned, he felt the best way to grow his business was to increase production and restructure the company.

Rockefeller brought his brother William into the business. They built a second refinery in Cleveland. The initial refinery was named Excelsior Works, and the new refinery operated under the name Standard Works. Each brother oversaw one refinery.

Rockefeller then brought John Andrews, the brother of Samuel Andrews, into the company. Rockefeller sent John Andrews to the Oil Region to manage the purchase of crude oil. He had strict instructions to telegram Rockefeller several times a day with the current price of crude oil. With this information, Rockefeller could monitor fluctuations. Prices fluctuated anywhere from $3 to $20 a barrel, so it was imperative that Rockefeller and his men stay on top of hourly prices and buy at the lowest possible rate. When prices plummeted, Rockefeller borrowed heavily from the banks to buy hefty quantities of cheaper crude oil. He then stored it in warehouses to sell when prices rose again.

As the business grew, Rockefeller turned his attention to marketing and export. By 1866, close to 70 percent of refined oil was shipped overseas

through wholesalers. Refineries would sell to
wholesalers at a low price, which, in turn, would
sell the oil at a higher price to overseas markets.
But Rockefeller pounced on the opportunity to cut
out the middleman and reap the profits of selling
abroad himself. He sent William to New York to set
up the office of Rockefeller and Company, which
would oversee the exportation of kerosene from
their Cleveland refineries. With his father's good
looks and charming personality, William was just the
salesman for the job.

## Flagler Enters the Business

After William moved from overseeing Standard
Works to setting up the New York office, Rockefeller
lured Henry M. Flagler, who owned a produce-
shipping business, to Rockefeller and Andrews.
Flagler had money of his own to invest, and he
enticed his wife's uncle, whiskey tycoon Stephen
V. Harkness, to invest as well. On March 4, 1867,
Rockefeller and Andrews was renamed Rockefeller,
Andrews and Flagler.

Whereas John Rockefeller was a quiet, reserved
man, Flagler was like Big Bill Rockefeller—outgoing
and social—but the two men agreed on their business

philosophy. Rockefeller viewed Flagler's energetic personality as a talent that would aid them in business. The two men became good friends, both at and outside work.

Flagler set out at once to use his charm and negotiation skills to chip away at the railroads. He was successful in persuading the Lake Shore Railroad to offer them lower shipping rates in exchange for a guarantee of 60 carloads of oil every day. The railroad was willing to secretly charge them $1.65 per barrel to ship refined oil back to New York, instead of the going rate of $2.40. Although Rockefeller, Andrews and Flagler was charged the posted rate, the difference was made up in rebates.

## A New Name

Rockefeller, Andrews and Flagler was thriving. On January 10, 1870, it became incorporated into a

**Rockefeller and Flagler**

Rockefeller and Flagler became successful partners and lifelong friends. Their desks backed up to each other's, and the men walked to work together every morning. They also attended the same church. Flagler noted, "A friendship founded on business is better than a business founded on friendship."[3]

joint-stock company under the new name Standard Oil Company with Rockefeller serving as president, William as vice president, and Flagler as both treasurer and secretary.

This new structure allowed the company to sell stock to investors who would profit when the company did. The investors provided the cash necessary for business expansion and development. Standard Oil, also called "The Standard," was born with $1 million worth of capital, and shares were valued at $100 each. Rockefeller, his brother William, Flagler, Andrews, and Harkness, the original partners, held 80 percent of the company's 10,000 shares and therefore retained control over business dealings. Under this new corporation, Standard Oil Company was on its way to becoming an oil giant. ⌐

In 1867, Henry M. Flagler became one of Rockefeller's business partners.

*John and Cettie Rockefeller's children: from left,
Bessie, Alta, Edith, and John Jr.*

# THE STANDARD OCTOPUS

*I*n 1870, the United States was
experiencing an economic depression.
While other leaders of industry became cautious
in their business dealings, Rockefeller nonetheless
forged ahead. In later years, he would again use these

tactics of taking advantage of less-than-favorable market conditions.

## A SECRET SCHEME

A history of fluctuating crude oil prices, rail rate wars, and an overabundance of refineries had caused upheaval and chaos in the oil business. Rockefeller yearned to overhaul the industry and to bring order—and steady profits—to the business.

**Oil in the Air**

By 1866, Cleveland was home to at least 50 oil refineries. The foul smell of massive amounts of crude oil being processed at these facilities hung in the air on the outskirts of Cleveland. It was so strong that it tainted the taste of beer brewed at local breweries and soured milk.

So Rockefeller, together with his partners, began secretly discussing the idea of uniting the Cleveland refineries into one large organization. The size and power of such an entity would allow the partners to better compete with and possibly undercut refineries in the Pittsburgh, New York, and Oil Region areas. A large entity might even be able to control the market.

Before starting that plan, Tom Scott of the Pennsylvania Railroad suggested another idea to Rockefeller. Scott proposed the larger refineries in Pittsburgh, New York, and Cleveland unite with the railroads. Working together, they could regulate prices and shipping costs at rates that benefited those involved—and potentially crush those who were not. United, the companies would also set minimum production quotas, or amounts member refineries were required to produce. This would mean only the largest refineries would produce enough to be able to participate.

## THE SOUTH IMPROVEMENT COMPANY

"In some measure I have been associated with the most interesting people our country has produced, especially in business— men who have helped largely to build up the commerce of the United States, and who have made known its products all over the world. These incidents which come to my mind to speak of seemed vitally impor- tant to me when they happened, and they still stand out distinctly in my memory."[1]

—John D. Rockefeller, 1908

The means of uniting would be through the South Improvement Company. This vague entity was essentially a holding company—a company that has influence and control over other companies. A charter for the South Improvement Company was approved by the Pennsylvania legislature in 1871. Unlike most companies at the time, the South Improvement Company could legally operate across state lines. This gave the refiners and railroads the perfect way to form one giant group to control prices.

*Rockefeller at age 35*

The railroads agreed to give large rebates on shipping rates to the refineries that joined the South Improvement Company. In addition to rebates, members of the South Improvement Company would receive "drawbacks." These additional rebates were taken out of the full-price fees paid by nonmember companies. Nonmember refineries would not only be forced to pay more for shipping their barrels, but some of that money would go directly to the member companies—potentially their competition. That meant any refiners that did not join would soon be forced out of business.

The South Improvement Company was a cutthroat business venture, and all those involved were sworn to secrecy. Describing the company, one biographer wrote, "Of all the devices for the extinction of competition, this was the cruelest and most deadly yet conceived by any group of American industrialists."[2] But Rockefeller did not see it as immoral or criminal. He believed unification of larger refineries would bring order and stability to the chaotic oil business. As he wrote to Cettie, "A man who succeeds in life must sometimes go against the current."[3]

## Buying Out the Competition

As the railroads and refiners negotiated terms in New York, Rockefeller returned to Cleveland where he began buying out the competition. He calmly gave Cleveland refineries two choices: fold their business into Standard Oil in exchange for stock or cash, or be bankrupted by the rebate system. If they chose to fold their business, Rockefeller urged them to take stock, and those who took cash often complained later that they had been cheated. He further complicated matters for his competitors by offering stock to local bankers. Refiners who refused to sell to him would now find difficulty securing loans with the bankers in Rockefeller's control.

Rockefeller's younger brother Frank was a partner at a competing Cleveland refinery and refused to sell. Rockefeller tried to reason with Frank, explaining that Standard intended to buy out all competitors in Cleveland. "Those who refuse will be crushed. If you don't sell your property to us, it will be valueless," he warned.[4] But Frank refused. When his business finally collapsed, Frank was very bitter with his older brother and remained so for the rest of his life. In the years to come, Frank spoke negatively about his brother to reporters.

Between February and March of 1872, Standard Oil bought out more

**Frank's Bitterness**

Although Rockefeller bailed out his brother Frank from several bad business decisions, Frank remained bitter about the ruination of his oil refinery business due to his older brother's massive buyout of the Cleveland refineries. Later in his life, Frank had the bodies of his two deceased children removed from the family cemetery and reburied elsewhere so they would not have to lie in the same plot as John D. Rockefeller.

than 20 of its competitors. Rockefeller hired some competitors to work for Standard Oil. Later referred to as "The Cleveland Massacre," the campaign marked the end of competitive oil business in Cleveland.

## Public Uproar

Back in New York, negotiations continued between the railroads and the refiners. Although the men had sworn an oath of secrecy, news of the South Improvement Company scheme leaked out. Panic raced through the Oil Region and the public reacted fiercely. All-night meetings were held, and lengthy petitions were signed.

It was not the unification of the refiners and railroads that infuriated people, or even the rebates for members. What tipped people over the edge was the drawback system, funded by the smaller non-members' exorbitant shipping costs. Ida Tarbell, who later investigated and reported on Rockefeller's monopoly, explained, "The rebate system was considered illegal and unjust, but men were more or less accustomed to it. The drawback on other people's shipments was a new device, and it threw the Oil Regions into a frenzy of rage."[5]

## The Oil Region Fights Back

Oil producers in the Oil Region organized into the Petroleum Producers' Union. They immediately cut back drilling by two-thirds, reducing the supply to refineries. They also boycotted the South Improvement Company refineries as well as the railroads. Riots at rail yards prevented trains from leaving, further threatening the railroads' business.

The railroads scurried to appease the Oil Region and vowed, "No rebates, drawbacks, or other

### Robber Barons

Andrew Carnegie, J. P. Morgan, Jay Gould, and John D. Rockefeller were some of the men labeled by the public as robber barons. In medieval times, the term *robber baron* referred to feudal lords who charged tolls to ships carrying goods through their lands. This was considered to be a greedy and underhanded way of making money.

Feudalism was a social and economic system that typically granted land in exchange for military service. Kings needed armored knights to fight for and protect their kingdoms. In exchange for large holdings of land, called feuds, barons provided the king with these warrior knights. The barons then leased portions of their feud to knights. In turn, these knights leased sections of their land to yeomen. This structure continued to the very lowest of their society's rank, the serfs. Every man owed money or military service to the man above him.

By the time of the Industrial Revolution, the term *robber baron* had come to describe the captains of industry who had made enormous amounts of money from their business or industry. Usually, these fortunes were made using unfair business practices and through underpayment of their workers.

arrangements of any character shall be made or allowed."[6] In addition, the Pennsylvania legislature approved a bill that revoked the charter of the South Improvement Company, causing the holding company to crumble.

Overnight, the name John D. Rockefeller—widely known in Cleveland but rather unknown elsewhere in the country—became synonymous with greed and corruption. Rockefeller had become a monster in the eyes of the US public. The newspapers dubbed his company "an octopus."[7] He was also branded as a robber baron—a businessman who uses questionable practices to shut out competition and dominate the market.

Rockefeller made no public comment about the accusations. He faced the public scrutiny with the same calm, confident manner that he exercised daily. He later defended his actions, stating, "It was right. I knew it as a matter of conscience. It was right between me and my God."[8] He never showed regret for his involvement with the holding company and firmly believed his quest to unite the oil refineries into one well-managed corporation was noble and honest.

## A NEW PLAN

Although the South Improvement Company was now gone, Rockefeller had successfully bought out the vast majority of his competitors in Cleveland. In so doing, he claimed 25 percent of the country's refinery production. He and Flagler still wanted the company to grow, though, and came up with a plan to increase that number. In April 1872, they proposed refiners join together in a confederation named the National Refiners' Association. A board would govern the confederation. It would also purchase crude oil, allot each refinery an amount determined by a quota, and secure uniform rates with the railroads.

This time, oil refiners and producers took interest. Jacob J. Vandergraft and John D. Archbold, leaders themselves in the refining business, joined the association. Rockefeller was chosen as president,

**Another Encounter with the Clark Brothers**

One of the Cleveland refineries Rockefeller purchased was Clark, Payne & Company. This company was co-owned by the Clark brothers, whom he had bought out years before when Andrews, Clark and Company dissolved. Rockefeller paid $400,000 cash for the company and offered Oliver H. Payne a position with the Standard Oil Company. He did not offer such positions to the Clark brothers, however.

a position that required him to tour each member's facilities in order to allot quotas for production. This allowed Rockefeller to gain knowledge of every leading refinery in the association. "That's what we were traveling around for, to know who and what they were and what they were good for," he said.[9]

When a four-year depression hit in 1873, the association collapsed. The price of crude oil plummeted, forcing some of the refineries out of business. The Standard Oil Company closed four of its six plants for a time but was still a profitable company. Payments made to shareholders were cut as well. But even though the oil business was suffering, Rockefeller was ramping up to take almost complete control of the world's oil refining industry.

An 1884 political cartoon depicts the Standard Oil Company
as an octopus crushing its competition.

*A woodcut depicts boring for oil in the Oil Region, 1865*

# ROCKEFELLER'S MONOPOLY

By 1873, Rockefeller had expanded his business to purchase oil refineries in Long Island, New York. Soon after, he acquired two large refineries in Titusville, Pennsylvania. The Standard soon expanded into other areas of the Oil

Region, and eventually the company controlled half of Pittsburgh's refining capacity.

Many refiners were adamantly against selling to Rockefeller. He gained control of these refineries, however, by quietly plotting with other refiners these companies trusted. Rockefeller struck deals with refinery owners such as John D. Archbold and Charles Pratt. They successfully purchased some of these holdout refineries. They then turned around and sold their newly expanded companies to Rockefeller.

With every oil refinery Standard Oil acquired, the more powerful the company became. Rockefeller could pressure the railroads into giving him better rates by threatening to end his business with them and ship via other routes instead. Affordable rates were crucial for Rockefeller because he had to transport crude oil and kerosene greater distances than the refineries on the Eastern seaboard.

By 1879, the Standard controlled 90 percent of the country's oil production. In 1884, the company was processing 96,000 barrels of crude oil a day, with storage tanks capable of holding several hundred thousand barrels of oil waiting to be refined. Rockefeller wanted to squeeze every bit of profit from the crude oil and began producing products from the petroleum by-products. Petroleum jelly, lubricants for machinery, the chemical cleaner benzine, and paraffin wax were all produced in plants on Standard's property.

This power and production established the Standard Oil Company as one of the most powerful monopolies in the history of the United States. Rockefeller's dream was becoming reality. He was 41 years old and quickly becoming the richest man in the nation.

### A Better Way to Transport Crude

The Tidewater Company was a well-financed company whose goal was to bypass the monopoly of Rockefeller. Although oil had been piped prior to the Tidewater campaign, it had only been over short distances. The pipeline Tidewater laid pumped crude oil over mountainous terrain and in much greater amounts than before.

The company began laying pipe over 109 miles (175 km) of land stretching from the Oil Region over the Allegheny Mountains to Williamsport, Pennsylvania. The initial pipeline lay atop the soil, but later, crews buried it under the surface to help protect it.

Prior to the pipelines, oil was transported from the oil fields by horse-drawn wagons driven by men known as teamsters. The teamsters moved the oil to railroad yards, where it was loaded onto flatcars and shipped to refineries. These men had to control their team of horses and pass through muddy, deep-rutted paths while carrying heavy, leaky oil barrels.

Pulling the heavy-laden wagons through miserable conditions was exhausting work for the horses. The pipeline was appealing because it ushered in a cleaner, safer way to move crude oil from wells to refineries.

By achieving his success, Rockefeller had also ruined countless small oil companies. The public viewed him and his cool attitude with contempt. Though his personal wealth was growing, he also became one of the most hated men in America.

## A NEW THREAT

In 1878, the Tidewater Company began laying pipeline that would allow crude oil to be pumped long distances from the oilfields to refineries. This new technology would drastically reduce the need for railroad shipments. After working so hard to secure preferred rates, and because the pipelines would pump crude oil to the coast refineries instead of to Cleveland, Rockefeller was determined to stop the oil pipelines from being built.

Rockefeller used his connections in the New York legislature to hamper bills that would award Tidewater rights to lay long-distance pipe, but Rockefeller's attempts ultimately failed. He instructed his men to begin buying farmland Tidewater hoped to lay pipe through. When news came that another group, the Equitable Petroleum Company, planned to lay pipe from the oil fields to Buffalo, New York—a plan that would effectively kill

Cleveland as a refining city—Rockefeller sent word to his agents, "Don't let them get a pipe to Buffalo."[1]

Rockefeller failed in his attempts to put an end to the oil pipelines. By mid-1879, oil was flowing from the oil fields to Williamsport, Pennsylvania, at a rate of 250 barrels an hour, 6,000 barrels a day.

### The Monopoly Grows

Rockefeller immediately sought to buy out the Tidewater Company, but his offer was refused. To keep a competitive edge on the refining business, he began laying his own pipeline to pump crude oil to Cleveland. By March 1880, he had four long-distance pipelines up and running. He gave his railroad partners cash subsidies to make up for some of the lost shipping, and eventually, he was able to buy out Tidewater. The Standard had weathered the pipeline storm and had come out on top yet again. But as the Standard's monopoly grew, so did public hostility. In addition, legal battles soon threatened the company.

In 1881, with the help of lawyer Samuel C. T. Dodd, Flagler devised a plan that would reorganize the Standard Oil Company. With a new structure, one centrally located office would operate refineries in other states. In order for the plan to work, each large refinery owned by the Standard Oil Company would essentially become its own corporation but would operate under direction of the central office. If the plan worked, many of the business investigations would end, and so would the Standard's legal troubles.

On January 2, 1882, Standard Oil Trust was founded. Forty separate corporations were joined under the umbrella of the trust and each corporation had one president. Rockefeller moved his family to New York City, the new headquarters of Standard Oil Trust.

In a brownstone on West Fifty-Fourth Street, the Rockefeller family led a simple life and stayed involved in the Baptist church. Rockefeller continued his practice of giving to the church.

Standard Oil Trust ventured into new waters. It purchased tin to manufacture its own oil cans, which damaged the canning companies in the process.

**Eliza's Death**

On March 28, 1889, Rockefeller's beloved mother, Eliza, died. She had never known of her husband's second wife or his double life as Dr. Levingston. Big Bill, now living in North Dakota on a ranch John had purchased for him, did not return to Cleveland for her funeral. This enraged John, who visited the reverend officiating at Eliza's funeral. As a result, the oration at the funeral, as well as Eliza's death certificate, announced that she had died a widow.

The octopus arms of Standard Oil Trust continued reaching for more profits and more power.

Rockefeller surrounded himself with talented and innovative executives. Although nearly all of them were older than he was, Rockefeller was respected and trusted as Standard Oil Trust's leader. Some of his indomitable force of executives included his brother William, Henry Flagler, John D. Archbold, Samuel C. T. Dodd, Oliver Payne, and Henry H. Rogers. By joining with Rockefeller, these men had become millionaires.

## Worldwide Markets

By the 1870s, Standard's kerosene could be found as far away as China, Japan, and the Middle East. Eighty-five percent of the world's kerosene supply was from Pennsylvania. Standard sold cheap kerosene lamps abroad, sometimes even giving them away free, to boost foreign consumption of kerosene. According to Rockefeller, "In many countries, we had to teach the people . . . to burn oil by making lamps for them; we packed the oil to be carried by camels or on the backs of runners in the most remote portions of the world; we adapted the trade to the needs of strange folk."[2]

## STRESSFUL TIMES

In the 1880s, the discovery of substantial oil reserves in the Baku region of Russia near the Caspian Sea gave Standard Oil Trust its first real European competitor. Standard reacted by exporting kerosene to Asia, but its stronghold on the market had taken a hit.

Perhaps triggered by stress, Rockefeller developed alopecia, a disease that causes one to lose all hair on the body, including eyebrows and eyelashes. Rockefeller was a man who had always been careful about his appearance and he began wearing wigs.

But there was more trouble for Rockefeller. In 1881, journalist and reformer Henry Demarest Lloyd published an article in the *Atlantic Monthly* that spoke out strongly against Standard Oil Trust. Lloyd criticized the company for selfishly crushing competitors in order to create a business giant. The investigative journalist eventually published *Wealth against Commonwealth* in 1894. In it, he claimed Rockefeller and

### Rockefeller's Wigs

Although Rockefeller was nowhere near as flashy as his father, he prided himself on his appearance. When alopecia caused him to lose all the hair on his body, he purchased a series of wigs, each a bit longer than the next. He wore the wigs in rotation, to give the appearance that his hair was growing, and then had been cut. This practice caused political cartoonists to poke fun at him, often drawing the wigs a bit off center.

his company were the epitome of the type of self-interested monopolies that negatively influenced the US economy and even democracy. These exposés were examples of a type of investigate journalism called muckraking. During this time, Standard Oil's business practices were investigated by the government.

Adding to Rockefeller's frustrations, muckraking journalist Ida Tarbell wrote a series of articles about Rockefeller and Standard Oil Trust that was published in *McClure's Magazine* in 1902. The groundbreaking work, entitled *History of the Standard Oil Company*, exposed the ruthless tactics used by the titan company to destroy smaller oil businesses. The installments were later published as a best-selling book, which helped further fuel public hatred toward Rockefeller. Things were about to change for Rockefeller and his business, but it would certainly not be the end of the oil tycoon.

**An Important Work**

In 1999, the *New York Times* published a list of "The Top 100 Works of Journalism in the United States in the 20th Century." The works were chosen by professors at New York University, who ranked Ida Tarbell's book *History of the Standard Oil Company* number five. Ms. Tarbell's father had been a barrel maker in the Oil Region who was bankrupted by Rockefeller.

Muckraking journalist Ida Tarbell published articles about
Rockefeller that greatly damaged his public image.

*By the time Rockefeller retired in 1911,*
*he had amassed an enormous personal fortune.*

# ROCKEFELLER THE
# PHILANTHROPIST

Beginning in the late 1800s, federal legislators started passing antitrust legislation. At the time, businesses were joining together to form large trusts, such as Standard Oil Trust. The antitrust regulations intended to promote free trade by prohibiting any one business from forming a monopoly. By limiting monopolies, competition between businesses would be encouraged, which could help keep prices low and protect consumers.

The Sherman Antitrust Act, passed in 1890, was the first piece of federal antitrust legislation. The legislation was the basis for a 1904 Supreme Court ruling that ordered the breakup of a railroad trust. And on May 15, 1911, the US Supreme Court declared Standard Oil Trust to be in violation of the Sherman Antitrust Act. The corporation was forced to dissolve into more than 30 companies that had to operate independently of each other.

Although the decision dealt Standard a heavy blow, it did not devastate the company. The advent and popularity of the automobile—which created a new need for petroleum—had set Standard's sales ablaze. Sources vary, but when Rockefeller officially retired in 1911

"The best philanthropy, the help that does the most good and the least harm, the help that nourishes civilization at its very root . . . is not what is usually called charity. It is, in my judgment, the investment of effort or time or money, carefully considered with relation to the power of employing people at a [profitable] wage, to expand and develop the resources at hand, and to give opportunity for progress and healthful labour where it did not exist before. No mere money-giving is comparable to this in its lasting and beneficial results."[1]

—John D. Rockefeller, *Random Reminiscences of Men and Events*

*A Standard Oil filling station in 1915*

at age 72, he was worth between $200 and $300 million. As Rockefeller's dividend payments from stocks skyrocketed and his wealth multiplied, he became a billionaire.

## A Generous Man

Rockefeller was greatly influenced by another captain of industry. Andrew Carnegie had amassed a fortune in the steel industry, and at one point, Carnegie was even wealthier than Rockefeller. Carnegie believed it was the duty of the wealthy to donate large sums of money to charitable causes during their lifetimes instead of leaving their fortunes to be spent by their heirs. He believed, "The man who dies thus rich dies disgraced."[2] Carnegie gave millions of dollars to fund more than 2,500 public libraries as well as schools and music halls.

While Rockefeller was growing his business, he also turned his attention to dispersing the money he earned. All his life, he had faithfully donated to the Baptist church and other charitable organizations as he saw fit. He believed God had given him the gift to make money, and it was his duty to use that gift to help humanity.

In May 1889, Rockefeller agreed to donate $600,000 of the $1 million needed to fund a Baptist college in Chicago—the University of Chicago. Frederick T. Gates, an articulate young Baptist minister, served as the fund-raiser for the college and sold the idea to Rockefeller. The aging oil business titan decided he needed help finding causes deserving of donations from his vast fortune.

## GATES HELPS ROCKEFELLER HELP OTHERS

In 1891, Gates was hired as Rockefeller's investment manager and philanthropic adviser. He was given the responsibility of researching

both investment and donation opportunities
and advised Rockefeller about both. Rockefeller
received hundreds of letters daily requesting money.
Rockefeller was not opposed to giving; however,
he wanted to give through an organization, not to
individuals for use at their discretion.

As a result of Gates's careful research, Rockefeller
invested in ore deposits in the Mesabi Iron Range of
Minnesota. Before he finally sold his interest in the
iron range to J. P. Morgan, a wealthy and powerful
financier, the investment had brought him more
than $50 million in profit.

Rockefeller's wealth was growing faster than he
could donate it. Gates once advised Rockefeller,
"Your fortune is rolling up, rolling up like an
avalanche! . . . You must distribute it faster than
it grows! If you do not, it will crush you and your
children and your children's children."[3] Gates felt
the most efficient way to dole out donations was to
set up charitable trusts. These trusts would donate
Rockefeller's money to areas such as education,
medicine, religion, and others.

First, Gates proposed the creation of a US medical
research facility at which doctors and researchers
would seek cures for diseases such as tuberculosis,

diphtheria, and typhoid. The Koch Institute for Infectious Diseases in Berlin, Germany, and the Pasteur Institute in Paris, France, had greatly elevated medical knowledge in Europe. The Rockefeller medical research facility, named the Rockefeller Institute for Medical Research, began operating in 1901. In 1907, following an outbreak of meningitis in New York, the institute's director Simon Flexner developed a serum to treat the disease. The institute distributed the serum free of charge to the public, potentially saving thousands of lives.

## Rockefeller's Medical Institute

In 1901, following the death of his grandson from scarlet fever, Rockefeller founded the first institution in the United States devoted solely to medical research. Incorporated on June 14, 1901, the Rockefeller Institute for Medical Research assembled a team of doctors and researchers who worked toward understanding diseases and infections, as well as their cures.

In its initial stages, the institute awarded grants for research studies. For two years it was housed in a temporary location before Rockefeller opened permanent laboratories in New York City on the site of a former farm. In addition to the laboratories, the Rockefeller Hospital was established in 1910. This allowed doctors to research diseases both in the laboratory and study them as they treated patients. Some of the first diseases researched at the Rockefeller Institute were polio, heart disease, and diabetes. It became a model for future medical research centers.

The institute's first major medical contribution was the discovery of a cure for meningitis. To date, the institute, now renamed the Rockefeller University, has contributed to 23 Nobel Prizes. It is one of the world's leading research centers.

In 1903, Gates helped Rockefeller establish the
General Education Board. Rockefeller's only son,
John Jr., also helped establish the board, which built
high schools throughout the South and provided
free instruction on improving education. It was
specifically intended to improve the education of
African Americans.

### Fighting Hookworm

In 1909, John Jr. convinced Rockefeller to
join the fight against a public health concern in
the South. The Rockefeller Sanitary Commission
was initiated with $1 million to put an end to
hookworm, a parasite that enters the body through
the skin, often through bare feet. People infected
with hookworm become weak and sluggish, and if
untreated, could be vulnerable to serious infection
and brain damage.

Dr. Charles Stiles discovered that what appeared
to be laziness or mental challenges in some southern
children was actually the result of hookworm
infections. The treatment was a 50-cent dose
of thymol and Epsom salts. But until Gates and
Rockefeller became involved, few would listen to
Dr. Stiles.

The Rockefeller Sanitary Commission sent teams of doctors to southern states to educate the public on the significance of sanitation. They preached the importance of wearing shoes year-round. The commission sent out "health trains," or traveling exhibitions, with microscopes that people could use to view hookworm eggs. Rural southerners lined up to look through these technological tools. After five years, close to 500,000 people were cured of hookworm. By 1913, the campaign spread to 52 countries on six continents and cured millions of people.

## THE ROCKEFELLER FOUNDATION

Rockefeller continued giving and set up a formal way to do so. Just like he believed that a large oil corporation would be most successful in the oil business, he wanted to establish a large foundation to effectively distribute his wealth. The Rockefeller Foundation, chartered by the state of New York in 1913, operated as a corporation run by executives and trustees. John Jr.

**Treating Hookworm**

During the campaign to fight hookworm, doctors discovered that nearly half the people they tested in the first year were infected. Within five years, they treated nearly 500,000 people. Gates boasted, "It has been reduced to one of the minor infections of the south, perhaps the most easily and universally recognized and cured of all."[4]

served as its president, and Gates was one of the nine trustees. Its goal was to administer grants, or funds, in large amounts to organizations that would aid humankind. Rockefeller gave $100 million to the foundation its first year.

By 1919, Rockefeller had donated more than $350 million to charitable causes. By the 1920s, the Rockefeller Foundation had become the largest grant-making foundation in the world, and Rockefeller was established as the most generous philanthropist in US history.

Universities and medical schools such as Johns Hopkins, Harvard, Yale, Columbia, and the University of Chicago were recipients of Rockefeller money. Medical research funded by Rockefeller helped unlock treatments and cures for scarlet fever, malaria, and yellow fever.

The man who had once been viewed by the public as a greedy monster was now a public servant. Rockefeller was helping to save millions of lives through his charitable deeds and forever changing the future of medicine and science. Although Standard Oil Trust earned him the hatred of the American people, its profits funded the foundation dedicated to improving countless lives worldwide.

*Frederick T. Gates, seated, and Simon Flexner, the first director
of the Rockefeller Institute for Medical Research*

*Rockefeller in 1930*

# THE ROCKEFELLER LEGACY

*L*ike his mother before him, Rockefeller
instilled in his children the importance
of giving to the church and leading a disciplined,
Christian life. Throughout his life, Rockefeller
abstained from drinking alcohol, smoking,

gambling, and card playing, all of which he considered sinful.

Bessie, Alta, Edith, and John Jr. never visited their father's offices or refineries. It was important to Rockefeller that his children learn the values of thrift and saving, as he had as a child. He required each to keep an account book in which they recorded the money they earned from chores such as gardening, sharpening pencils, and killing flies.

The Rockefeller children grew up wearing hand-me-down clothing, including John Jr., who wore his sister's dresses until he was eight. Even Cettie opted to sew patches on her dresses instead of buying new ones. Although the Rockefellers could have easily afforded bicycles for each child, Cettie decided it would be good for them to learn to share one.

The children were expected to be on time for meals and morning prayers and were fined for being late. Their mother did not believe in waste, and that included time. Every Sunday, the family attended church

### Changing His Reputation

As he aged, Rockefeller began carrying shiny, new nickels in his pockets that he would give to children he met in public. Receiving one of these coins from the wealthiest man in the nation was like getting a small token from a movie star. Along with the nickels, the children received a lesson in savings and compound interest, as Rockefeller told them that the nickel represented one year's interest on a dollar. This practice was encouraged by public relations experts hired to help Rockefeller redeem the family's tarnished reputation.

*Rockefeller, left, walks with his son, John Jr., in New York City in March 1915*

prayer meetings and Sunday school. Evenings were spent singing hymns. If the children had spare time, they were allowed to read only from the Bible.

The Rockefellers did not allow their children to mingle in public society. They were schooled at home, and the only social functions they attended were at the Baptist church. Their friends were restricted to the children of church acquaintances.

But despite this sheltered life, the family enjoyed time together at their summer home where Rockefeller taught them to swim and ride bicycles. He eagerly joined the children, playing blind man's bluff, giving them rides on his back, or telling them fairy tales.

## JOHN ROCKEFELLER JR.

While Rockefeller was a loving and devoted father to all of his children, his only son, John Jr., held a special place in his heart. John Jr. became heir to the Rockefeller fortune, and his father fully expected him to follow into the world of business.

John Jr. entered Brown University in Providence, Rhode Island, in 1893. After spending a childhood isolated from much of the outside world, John Jr. was free to experience the pleasures of life, such as watching football games and ballroom dancing. His mother, nervous that other young men might introduce him to smoking and drinking, disapproved of her son's social life.

Following graduation, John Jr. went to work for the Standard Oil Company. But, unlike his father, he found little pleasure in it. He wished, instead, to work in philanthropy like Gates.

Although Rockefeller hoped his son would follow in his footsteps, he did respect his son's bargaining skills. John Jr. had demonstrated them during a messy strike at a Colorado mine in 1914. Workers at the Rockefeller-owned coal mine had been striking for more than a year when local militia attacked the camp where the workers lived with their families. Later called the Ludlow Massacre, the event left 18 people dead, including women and children. The public was outraged by the event, and much of the hatred

## Rockefeller Center

Located in the heart of Manhattan, New York City, Rockefeller Center is a series of commercial buildings financed solely and constructed by John Jr. during the 1930s. Originally, the project was to be financed by a group of investors. But those plans were changed after the stock market crash of 1929, which devastated markets worldwide and caused great economic turmoil. John Jr. was suddenly faced with the decision of abandoning the project or paying for it himself.

He moved forward with the plans. The project became the largest private construction project undertaken in the modern era. Fourteen original office complexes were erected. Each featured the bold lines and streamlined forms of the then-popular Art Deco style.

Rockefeller Center is home to Radio City Music Hall, NBC Studios, and Fox News. The popular live television show *Saturday Night Live* is filmed at the GE Building located at 30 Rockefeller Plaza. "30 Rock," as it is called, is the centerpiece of the Rockefeller Plaza and is also the location of the offices of the Rockefeller Group.

Every winter since 1933, a large Christmas tree is set up and lit during the Rockefeller Center Tree Lighting Ceremony. This annual event attracts throngs of visitors who come to see the illuminated tree and to ice-skate at the Rockefeller Ice Skating Rink.

was poured out on Rockefeller and his son. John
Jr. spoke publicly, negotiated with the strikers, and
was involved in the court hearings following the
massacre. He did a great deal to help restore the
family's name. But after this event, John Jr. took a
lesser role in his father's company and a greater role
in his father's philanthropic dealings.

John Jr. resigned from the position of vice
president of the Standard Oil Company in 1910
and then dedicated his life to philanthropic work.
He financed the building of Rockefeller Center at
30 Rockefeller Plaza in New York City. As a result
of this project, many construction workers were
employed throughout the Great Depression, a time
of worldwide economic hardship during the late
1920s and throughout the 1930s. He gave money to
medicine and the arts and funded the creation of
several national parks in such areas as the redwood
forests of California, the Shenandoah Valley in
western Virginia, the Great Smoky Mountains
between Tennessee and North Carolina, and the
Grand Tetons in Wyoming. He also provided
land and improvements for Acadia National Park
in Maine.

*The GE Building was built in the Art Deco architectural style and is part of the Rockefeller Center complex.*

## The Rockefellers through the Years

As John Jr. took over work at the Rockefeller Foundation, Rockefeller and Cettie moved to a country estate in Pocantico Hills in Westchester County, New York, where Rockefeller indulged his hobbies of golfing and landscape gardening. He was now aging into a thin, withered, elderly man.

In 1915, Cettie passed away. She was buried in the family burial plot in Lake View Cemetery in Cleveland. Rockefeller once addressed the Euclid Avenue Baptist Church, stating that, "People tell me I have done much in my life. I know I have worked hard. But the best thing I ever accomplished and the thing that has given me the greatest happiness was to win Cettie Spelman. I have had but one sweetheart and am thankful to say I still have her."[1]

## Final Days

Although Rockefeller was convinced that golf and a simple, healthy diet would help him reach his goal of living to be 100 years old, the oil titan died a few years short of living a full century. Rockefeller suffered a heart attack at the age of 97 and died on May 23, 1937, just six weeks before his ninety-eighth birthday. The following day, Standard Oil companies throughout the world stopped work for five minutes to honor their founder.

### Aiding Women's Education

In 1881, the Atlanta Baptist Female Seminary was established as the first all African-American women's seminary in Atlanta, Georgia. Rockefeller first heard the founders speak in Cleveland on a fund-raising tour in 1882. Rockefeller donated money to the school, which was renamed the Spelman Seminary, in honor of his wife and her parents, who had always supported the antislavery movement. It is now Spelman College.

Rockefeller was laid to rest in Cleveland between the two most important women in his life: his mother, Eliza, and his wife, Cettie. Newspaper obituaries focused on his giving rather than on his tainted reputation. One editor hailed him as "the world's greatest philanthropist and organizer in the science of giving." Another noted that, "Because of him the world is a better place in which to live."[2]

**Continuing Rockefeller's Philanthropy**

Following Hurricane Katrina in 2005, the Rockefeller Foundation helped develop the Unified New Orleans Plan (UNOP), which focuses on providing housing, services, health care, and improving the community. The UNOP has provided millions of dollars to help New Orleans's reconstruction efforts.

## An Enduring Legacy

Despite the tarnished reputation he gained from his work with Standard Oil Company, it is impossible to ignore the fact that Rockefeller was a genius at making money. He was a pioneer in the oil business and revolutionized the way in which corporations functioned. The man behind one of the first modern corporations in the United States also helped Americans determine what they believed to be fair and unfair in business practices—and whether the government should step in to regulate these businesses.

But Rockefeller's influence also left an indelible mark on modern philanthropy. The legacy that Rockefeller left behind was a family dedicated to serving humanity through giving and public service. Rockefeller was a devoted grandfather and took pleasure in seeing his grandchildren being taught to be fiscally responsible yet generous. Of John Jr.'s six children, John D. Rockefeller III established the Lincoln Center for the Performing Arts in New York, Nelson served as governor of New York and vice president of the United States, Laurance was a conservationist and a developer, Winthrop became governor of Arkansas, and David became a banker and would later serve as chairman of Chase Manhattan Bank. Abby, John Jr.'s only daughter, created Greenacre Park in New York City in 1971. It contained a waterfall to provide New Yorkers with a small piece of nature in the big city.

The following Rockefeller generations have created their own philanthropic foundations to respond to the important issues of their time. Rockefeller's grandchildren created the Rockefeller Brothers Fund in 1940, and their children established the Rockefeller Family Fund in 1967. Both continue to be active philanthropic trusts.

**Going Green**

For more than 75 years, the formal gardens atop the roofs of certain Rockefeller Center buildings have delighted visitors and tenants. The architect believed the aesthetics, or the visual beauty, of the buildings should not include just the exterior walls.

In his own lifetime, Rockefeller donated approximately $540 million—more than $5 billion in today's dollars—to various humanitarian causes. The Rockefeller Foundation continues to give money to medical research and other humanitarian efforts, and scientific research continues at the Rockefeller University. John D. Rockefeller, the boy who so eagerly began his bookkeeping career earning a few dollars a week, became the wealthiest man in the United States and one of the most generous benefactors of all time. ⌐

Rockefeller's philanthropic endeavors continue to benefit those in need.

# TIMELINE

### 1839

John D. Rockefeller is born on July 8 near Richford, New York.

### 1855

On September 26, Rockefeller is hired at Hewitt and Tuttle, his first bookkeeping job.

### 1859

In spring, Maurice Clark and Rockefeller open their doors as a commission house.

### 1865

The partnership of Rockefeller and Andrews begins in February.

### 1867

Rockefeller brings brother William, John Andrews, and Henry Flagler into the business, which they rename Rockefeller, Andrews and Flagler.

### 1870

On January 10, Rockefeller, Andrews and Flagler is incorporated under the name Standard Oil Company.

## 1863

Andrews, Clark and Company, a small oil refinery, is born, entering Rockefeller into the oil business.

## 1864

Rockefeller and Laura Celestia Spelman are married on September 8 in her parents' living room.

## 1865

In February, Andrews, Clark and Rockefeller is dissolved; Rockefeller buys out the Clark brothers for $72,500.

## 1871

The Pennsylvania legislature approves the charter of the South Improvement Company.

## 1872

The National Refiners' Association is born in April.

## 1873

The National Refiners' Association collapses.

# TIMELINE

### 1878

The Tidewater Company begins laying pipeline from the Oil Region to Williamsport, Pennsylvania.

### 1882

On January 2, Standard Oil Trust is founded.

### 1889

Rockefeller pledges $600,000 in May to fund a Baptist college in Chicago.

### 1903

Rockefeller establishes the General Education Board.

### 1909

Through a $1 million donation, the Rockefeller Sanitary Commission begins the fight against hookworm in the South.

### 1911

On May 15, the US Supreme Court rules the Standard Oil Trust to be in violation of the Sherman Antitrust Act.

## 1891

Rockefeller hires Frederick T. Gates to help him organize his charitable giving.

## 1901

The Rockefeller Institute for Medical Research begins operation on June 14.

## 1902

Ida Tarbell's *History of the Standard Oil Company* is published, renewing public outrage at the Standard's business practices.

## 1913

The Rockefeller Foundation is chartered in New York State.

## 1919

Rockefeller's charitable donations reach $350 million.

## 1937

Rockefeller dies on May 23, just weeks short of his ninety-eighth birthday.

# ESSENTIAL FACTS

DATE OF BIRTH

July 8, 1839

PLACE OF BIRTH

Richford, New York

DATE OF DEATH

May 23, 1937

PARENTS

William Avery "Big Bill" Rockefeller and Eliza Davison Rockefeller

EDUCATION

Owego Academy, Clinton Street School, Central High School, Folsom's Commercial College

MARRIAGE

Laura Celestia "Cettie" Spelman (September 8, 1864)

CHILDREN

Elizabeth "Bessie," Alice, Alta, Edith, John Jr.

## CAREER HIGHLIGHTS

By 25, Rockefeller was owner of Cleveland's largest oil refinery. On January 10, 1870, Rockefeller became president of the Standard Oil Company. On January 2, 1882, Standard Oil Trust was founded with Rockefeller heading up the board of trustees.

## SOCIETAL CONTRIBUTIONS

Rockefeller contributed from his earnings to the Baptist church, medical research, and educational improvement. The Rockefeller Foundation was established in 1913 to administer large grants to organizations that would aid humankind. Rockefeller donated approximately $540 million—more than $5 billion in today's dollars—to various humanitarian causes during his lifetime.

## CONFLICTS

In 1902, investigative journalist Ida Tarbell's articles *History of the Standard Oil Company* were published. The series helped fuel the public's hatred of Rockefeller. On May 15, 1911, the Supreme Court declared the Standard Oil Trust to be in violation of the Sherman Antitrust Act.

## QUOTE

"The best philanthropy, the help that does the most good and the least harm, the help that nourishes civilization at its very root . . . is not what is usually called charity. It is, in my judgment, the investment of effort or time or money, carefully considered with relation to the power of employing people at a [profitable] wage, to expand and develop the resources at hand, and to give opportunity for progress and healthful labour where it did not exist before. No mere money-giving is comparable to this in its lasting and beneficial results."—*John D. Rockefeller*

# GLOSSARY

**alopecia**
A disease that causes all of one's hair to fall out.

**commodities**
Goods such as oil, grain, or gold that vary only slightly between producers.

**dividends**
Shares or rewards; in a business, dividends are often distributed to investors or shareholders out of a company's profits.

**drawbacks**
A system in which additional rebates are paid to companies that are members of a large group or corporation; the drawbacks are paid out of the full-price fees paid by nonmember companies.

**flimflam man**
A traveling salesman who often sells sham products or "miracle" cures.

**hookworm**
A parasite that enters the body through the skin and causes humans to feel lethargic and be anemic.

**Industrial Revolution**
A time spanning from the 1700s to the 1800s and later that included many developments in science and technology as machines and factories transformed business, society, and economies.

**kerosene**
An oil often burned in lamps to produce light.

**muckraking**
An often sensational type of journalism that exposed corruption or shady practices by businesses, the government, or individuals.

**oil derrick**
> A large piece of equipment used to drill for oil or other natural resources in the earth; an oil derrick consists of an upright stationary piece that supports the drilling equipment.

**petroleum**
> Crude oil; petroleum can be refined for use as fuel.

**philanthropy**
> Giving, especially of money, to help others.

**rebate**
> A return of a portion of a sum paid.

**refinery**
> A building or a plant that processes a product, such as crude oil.

**subsidy**
> Financial support.

**teamsters**
> Men who transported oil from the oil fields to the railroad stations by horse-drawn wagon.

**temperance**
> Abstinence from or limited use of alcohol.

**Underground Railroad**
> The system of homes and workers who secretly helped slaves from the southern states reach the free North or Canada.

**whaling**
> The business of hunting whales for meat and parts that can be made into products such as oil.

# ADDITIONAL RESOURCES

## SELECTED BIBLIOGRAPHY

Chernow, Ron. *Titan: The Life of John D. Rockefeller, Sr.* New York: Random, 1998. Print.

Hawke, David Freeman. *John D.: The Founding Father of the Rockefellers.* New York: Harper, 1980. Print.

Morris, Charles R. *The Tycoons: How Andrew Carnegie, John D. Rockefeller, Jay Gould, and J.P. Morgan Invented the American Supereconomy.* New York: Henry Holt, 2005. Print.

"People & Events: John D. Rockefeller Senior, 1839–1937." *The American Experience.* PBS Online, n.d. Web.

Rockefeller, John D. *Random Reminiscences of Men and Events.* New York: Doubleday, 1909. *The Project Gutenberg Ebook.* Web.

Weinberg, Steve. *Taking on the Trust: The Epic Battle of Ida Tarbell and John D. Rockefeller.* New York: Norton, 2008. Print.

## FURTHER READINGS

Laughlin, Rosemary. *John D. Rockefeller: Oil Baron and Philanthropist.* Greensboro, NC: Morgan Reynolds, 2004. Print.

McNeese, Tim. *The Robber Barons and the Sherman Antitrust Act: Reshaping American Business.* New York: Chelsea, 2009. Print.

Segall, Grant. *John D. Rockefeller: Anointed with Oil.* New York: Oxford University Press, 2001. Print.

## WEB LINKS

To learn more about John D. Rockefeller, visit ABDO Publishing Company online at **www.abdopublishing.com**. Web sites about John D. Rockefeller are featured on our Book Links page. These links are routinely monitored and updated to provide the most current information available.

## Places to Visit

**Drake Well Museum**
202 Museum Lane, Titusville, PA 16354
814–827–2797
www.drakewell.org
The Drake Well Museum, located at the site of Edwin Drake's first successful oil drill, offers educational tours, history camps, and lectures designed to introduce visitors to the development of the oil industry. It is also home to the Drake Well Museum Library, one of the largest collections of materials relating to the birth of the oil industry, and houses the largest collection of pictures illustrating the early days of the oil business.

**Kykuit, the Rockefeller Estate**
381 North Broadway, Sleepy Hollow, NY 10591
914–631–3992
www.hudsonvalley.org/content/view/12/42
Take a tour of the six-story home and gardens of John D. Rockefeller in the Hudson Valley. The estate was home to four generations of the Rockefeller family and includes Nelson Rockefeller's collection of sculpture and art.

**Rockefeller Center**
W Forty-Ninth Street & Fifth Avenue, New York, NY 10020
212–632–3975
www.rockefellercenter.com
Rockefeller Center, consisting of 19 buildings in Manhattan, New York, is home to NBC Studios and Radio City Music Hall, among other businesses and organizations. During the winter season, the Ice Skating Rink at Rockefeller Center offers ice-skating and skate rentals. Each year, a tree lighting ceremony is held for the tree at Rockefeller Center.

# Source Notes

**Chapter 1. Young Determination**
1. Ron Chernow. *Titan: The Life of John D. Rockefeller, Sr.* New York: Random, 1998. Print. 44.
2. Ibid.
3. Ibid. 45.
4. Ibid.
5. Ibid. 46.
6. David Freeman Hawke. *John D.: The Founding Father of the Rockefellers.* New York: Harper, 1980. Print. 20.

**Chapter 2. The Young Entrepreneur**
1. David Freeman Hawke. *John D.: The Founding Father of the Rockefellers.* New York: Harper, 1980. Print. 10.
2. Ron Chernow. *Titan: The Life of John D. Rockefeller, Sr.* New York: Random, 1998. Print. 19.
3. "People & Events: John D. Rockefeller Senior, 1839-1937." *The American Experience.* PBS Online, n.d. Web. 25 July 2009.
4. Ron Chernow. *Titan: The Life of John D. Rockefeller, Sr.* New York: Random, 1998. Print. 34–35.

**Chapter 3. The Savvy Businessman**
1. David Freeman Hawke. *John D.: The Founding Father of the Rockefellers.* New York: Harper, 1980. Print. 21.
2. Ron Chernow. *Titan: The Life of John D. Rockefeller, Sr.* New York: Random, 1998. Print. 49.
3. Ibid. 68.
4. David Freeman Hawke. *John D.: The Founding Father of the Rockefellers.* New York: Harper, 1980. Print. 29.

**Chapter 4. The Business of Oil**
1. Ron Chernow. *Titan: The Life of John D. Rockefeller, Sr.* New York: Random, 1998. Print. 68.
2. Ibid. 70.
3. Ibid. 77.
4. Ibid.
5. Ibid.
6. Ibid. 91.

**Chapter 5. Standard Oil Is Born**
 1. David Freeman Hawke. *John D.: The Founding Father of the Rockefellers.* New York: Harper, 1980. Print. 53.
 2. Ron Chernow. *Titan: The Life of John D. Rockefeller, Sr.* New York: Random, 1998. Print. 87.
 3. Daniel Yergin. *The Prize: The Epic Quest for Oil, Money & Power.* New York: Free Press, 2008. Print. 22.

**Chapter 6. The Standard Octopus**
 1. John D. Rockefeller. *Random Reminiscences of Men and Events.* New York: Doubleday, 1909. Preface. *The Project Gutenberg Ebook.* Web. 4 Aug. 2009.
 2. Daniel Yergin. *The Prize: The Epic Quest for Oil, Money & Power.* New York: Free Press, 2008. Print. 25.
 3. David Freeman Hawke. *John D.: The Founding Father of the Rockefellers.* New York: Harper, 1980. Print. 72.
 4. Charles D. Ellis and James R. Vertin. *Wall Street People: True Stories of the Great Barons of Finance, Volume 2.* New York: John Wiley & Sons, 2003. Print. 77.
 5. Ibid. 78.
 6. David Freeman Hawke. *John D.: The Founding Father of the Rockefellers.* New York: Harper, 1980. Print. 86.
 7. Ron Chernow. *Titan: The Life of John D. Rockefeller, Sr.* New York: Random, 1998. Print. 166.
 8. Charles D. Ellis and James R. Vertin. *Wall Street People: True Stories of the Great Barons of Finance, Volume 2.* New York: John Wiley & Sons, 2003. Print. 78.
 9. David Freeman Hawke. *John D.: The Founding Father of the Rockefellers.* New York: Harper, 1980. Print. 91.

**Chapter 7. Rockefeller's Monopoly**
 1. David Freeman Hawke. *John D.: The Founding Father of the Rockefellers.* New York: Harper, 1980. Print. 128.
 2. Ron Chernow. *Titan: The Life of John D. Rockefeller, Sr.* New York: Random, 1998. Print. 244.

## Source Notes Continued

**Chapter 8. Rockefeller the Philanthropist**

1. E. Richard Brown. *Rockefeller Medicine Men: Medicine and Capitalism in America*. Berkeley, CA: University of California, 1979. Print. 18.

2. Ron Chernow. *Titan: The Life of John D. Rockefeller, Sr.* New York: Random, 1998. Print. 313.

3. "People & Events: Frederick T. Gates, 1853-1929." *The American Experience*. PBS Online, n.d. Web. 17 Sept. 2010.

4. Ron Chernow. *Titan: The Life of John D. Rockefeller, Sr.* New York: Random, 1998. Print. 490–491.

**Chapter 9. The Rockefeller Legacy**

1. Ron Chernow. *Titan: The Life of John D. Rockefeller, Sr.* New York: Random, 1998. Print. 592.

2. Ibid. 675.

# INDEX

# INDEX CONTINUED

## About the Author

Susan E. Hamen is a full-time author and editor who finds
writing and editing children's books her most rewarding career
experiences. She has written educational books on a variety
of topics, including the Wright brothers, the Lewis and Clark
expedition, and Pearl Harbor. Hamen delights in living immersed
in the changing seasons of her home state, Minnesota, along
with her husband and two young children. In her spare time, she
can usually be found reading, canning, sewing, or working on
perfecting her apple pie crust.

## Photo Credits

AP Images, cover, 3, 13, 32, 35, 74, 84, 90, 95, 99 (bottom);
Rockefeller Archive Center, 6, 14, 18, 23, 24, 31, 41, 52, 83, 96
(top), 97, 99 (top); Library of Congress, 10; Time Life Pictures/
Contributor/Getty Images, 42; Bettmann/Corbis, 51, 64, 86;
Hulton Archive/Stringer/Getty Images, 55, 76, 96 (bottom), 98;
Stock Montage/Contributor/Getty Images, 63; Frances Benjamin
Johnston/Corbis, 73